MacBook
SENIORS GUIDE

A STEP-BY-STEP MANUAL FOR THE
NON-TECH-SAVVY TO MASTER YOUR
MACBOOK AIR AND PRO IN NO TIME

John Halbert

TABLE OF CONTENTS

INTRODUCTION

This book clearly explains how seniors can get started with the Mac, as well as other ideas for customizing the Dock so that its appearance appeals to you. Some of the tasks you want to complete on your Mac will necessitate the use of the internet, which is why this book teaches you how to connect to Wi-Fi. Not only that, but advice on selecting the best browser is also provided. We chose the Safari browser because it was created by Apple. All of this is done to make your internet experience as enjoyable as possible.

The book also includes some pointers to help you navigate your Mac as easily and quickly as possible. It is my hope that by the end of this book, you will have gained a lot of knowledge and confidence in navigating your Mac.

Just as people's lifestyles, travel habits, and eating habits change, so does the evolution of computers. Apple laptop computers first appeared in 1991. There have been numerous models and naming conventions over the years. Apple's first machine was known as the PowerBook 100. It had a trackball, a set-back keyboard, and a palm rest built in. In 1994, the PowerBook 500 and the PowerBook G3 were released. Each new version released had significant improvements. Apple released the iBook G3 in 1999, followed by the PowerBook Titanium G4 in early 2001. Apple first introduced the MacBook Pro and Air in 2006, with several updates since then.

The Apple MacBook laptop is one of Steve Jobs' most significant designs. The MacBook laptop line made its debut in January 2006. Laptops were not as common at the time as they are now, and most people who had access to computers used desktop computers. Laptop prices began to fluctuate around this time. The price decrease was due to the small size, low cost, and low-power systems used in the production of laptops.

Manufacturers began using low-cost materials to make laptops in order to keep prices affordable for price-conscious consumers. Apple, on the other hand, raised their standards by producing a better laptop that sold for a higher price on the market. The groundbreaking M1 chip, which was specifically designed for Mac laptops, was responsible for the higher standard. The M1 chip has a high performance per watt, allowing users to access faster machine learning capabilities. Furthermore, the battery life of Mac laptops and computers has been doubled. Users can also access a wide range of applications, as well as other outstanding features.

MacBook laptops also included the 'touch' feature for easier control and navigation. The mouse was phased out with the introduction of the touch system. Other players have followed suit, but the MacBooks are far ahead. When it comes to laptops, the MacBook has been the most influential over the last half-decade. Not only does its price remain high, but it also has other characteristics that distinguish it. For example, it lacks common components with other laptops, such as HDMI and SD card readers. Apple has also begun to produce laptops with non-removable batteries.

Let's get started.

CHAPTER 1
A BRIEF HISTORY OF THE MACBOOK SINCE 2006

Apple launched the Macbook in 2006. It was the first time they launched a laptop that used Mac OS X, the company's operating system. The company had announced in 2005 that it would be switching to Intel processors. The previous PowerBook and iBook brands sold by Apple were changed to reflect the new brand. The MacBook Air (2008-present) and the MacBook Pro (2006-present) are the two models of the Macbook. From 2006 to 2012, and again from 2015 to

2019, the MacBook laptop line was divided into two distinct lines. Users could switch between the two lines at various points in time.

It began with a design that was similar to the previous iBook and PowerBook versions. The MacBook line then transitioned to a unibody aluminum construction, which was first seen in the MacBook Air. To make things even better, this new version included a black plastic keyboard similar to the one found on the current MacBook Air, which was inspired by the recessed keyboard found on the first polycarbonate MacBooks. The now-standard keyboard, with black keys on a gleaming aluminum frame, connects all MacBooks.

Instead of a moving-parts lock, a magnet was used to keep the lid closed on the polycarbonate MacBook. In comparison to the previous MacBook, the new compact range solders or glues all of these components together. All Macbooks come with a lit-up keyboard.

The MacBook Air is Apple's most affordable laptop computer to date. The MacBook is consistently regarded as the best ultraportable device.

In 2017, Apple made significant changes to the MacBook Air. It now has a faster 1.8 GHz processor rather than a slower 1.6 GHz processor.

On November 10, 2020, Apple announced that the MacBook Air will be equipped with Apple's new M1 system on a chip, making it quieter. The new Air does not include a fan. According to the company, its laptop outperforms most Intel laptops currently on the market.

A high-end MacBook Pro from Apple can have either a 13-inch or a 16-inch screen. In October of that year, the new 13-inch MacBook Pro was released. It has a touch-sensitive OLED strip, and the power button now has a Touch ID sensor built in. It also has four USB-C Thunderbolt 3-compatible ports. A 13-inch MacBook Pro with function keys and only two USB-C/Thunderbolt 3 ports are also available. The basic MacBook Pro now has a Touch Bar and quad-core processors, but it still only has two USB-C / Thunderbolt 3 ports. When the next MacBook Pro was released in May 2020, it featured a scissor mechanism keyboard (dubbed "Magic Keyboard") and an Escape button that made a sound when pressed.

Apple released it on November 10, 2020. However, Apple customers can still purchase MacBook Pros with Intel processors. With a fan, Apple's M1 SoC-equipped MacBook Pro may be able to match or outperform its Intel-based competitors. The M1 model has a 13-inch display, two Thunderbolt ports, and up to 16 GB of RAM. The Intel Pro version has only one Thunderbolt port and less RAM (RAM).

Apple held an online event on October 18, 2021, to showcase the new 14-inch and 16-inch MacBook Pros.

The M1 Pro and M1 Max are based on Apple's first ARM-based systems on chips for professionals. The previous generation had a few issues, and some of them have been addressed in this one. Traditional function keys, for example, were reintroduced in place of the Touch Bar, an HDMI 2.0 port was added, an SDXC reader was added, and MagSafe charging was added. It has a Liquid Retina screen with a notch, ProMotion with a variable refresh rate of 120Hz, a 1080p webcam, and Wi-Fi 6. It also has three Thunderbolt 4 ports, a six-speaker sound system with Dolby Atmos support, and a third 6K monitor port. [11] The 16-inch model is powered by a 140W GaN power supply and supports USB-C Power Delivery 3.1. It also has a MagSafe fast-charging port, which is required because the machine's USB-C ports can only deliver 100W.

CHAPTER 2

DIFFERENT MODELS, PRICES, AND SPECS

MacBook Air

It is the lightest and thinnest notebook that is powered by the M1 chip. As Apple's first system on a chip, the M1 chip has security features, the processor, GPU, I/O, and RAM all in just one chip. Please note that the M1 chip was custom-made for Mac. This silicon chip is very small, though extremely efficient as compared to

Apple's previous chips. This is because the chip is built on a five-nanometer processor.

The MacBook was updated in November 2020, and it now starts at $999. It has a 7 or 8-core GPU, an 8-core CPU, and a machine learning neural engine with 16 cores. The MacBook Air comes in two variants, each 13.3-inch with a 2560 x 1600 display. The first, which costs $999, features the M1 chip with 7-core graphics and 256 GB of storage. The other costs $1,249 and includes the M1 chip with 8-core graphics and 512 GB of storage.

The MacBook Air was one of the first Apple mac laptops to use Apple silicon. Following the transition, the MacBook Air had a slimmer, fanless design, significantly improved performance, and a longer battery life. The MacBook Air's battery life is quite impressive. When you use the Apple television application, you can watch up to 18 hours of video and surf the internet for about 15 hours. In 2022, Apple announced that it would release a new and improved MacBook Air.

Other laptops have a fan to help with cooling. The MacBook Air, on the other hand, has an aluminum heat spreader that disperses heat, allowing for silent operation. When compared to previous MacBook Air models, the only internal change is the addition of an aluminum heat spreader. Because Apple does not use Intel processors in the MacBook Air, but rather its own custom silicon, it is more likely that the laptop will be updated more frequently in the future.

Most previous MacBook Air updates were internal rather than external. The laptop maintains its tapered, wedge-shaped aluminum body. It also has a 13-inch Retina display with thin bezels. It also includes a large Force Touch Trackpad. The MacBook Air is available in silver, gold, and space gray.

The 13-inch screen features new P3 wide color support, allowing for more vivid and realistic color projection. It provides a true tone that improves the strategic match between the white balance of the screen and the ambient lighting. It provides a more natural viewing experience, reducing the likelihood of eyestrain. This laptop has a maximum brightness of 400 nits.

The MacBook Air has a magical keyboard with a refined scissor mechanism. These features provide up to one millimeter of key travel, resulting in a more stable key feel. The MacBook Air laptop includes a 720-pixel facetime HD camera that works with the M1 chip to improve picture quality, reduce noise, and provide a wider dynamic range.

The keyboard on the MacBook Air has been slightly modified to improve usability. Apple has included function keys for "Spotlight search," "Do not disturb," and dictation. A new "emoji Fn key" is also included on the keyboard. The keyboard also has backlit keys that are activated by an ambient light sensor, allowing them to light up in dark environments. The security features on the MacBook Air are also exceptional. When you want to unlock your Mac or make purchases, you could use your touch ID fingerprint sensor instead of your password. The Secure Enclave protects the Touch ID by keeping your personal information and fingerprint data safe.

Wi-Fi 6 or 802.11ax and Bluetooth 5.0 are supported by the MacBook Air. It has two Thunderbolt 3 or USB 4 ports and can support up to 6000 external displays. The MacBook Air includes stereo speakers with wide stereo sound support, a 3.5mm headphone jack, and a three-microphone array.

The MacBook Pro

In 2016, Apple introduced two models of the MacBook Pro. One was with a touch bar, whereas the other had none. The updated MacBook Pro without a touch bar completely replaced an earlier version of the MacBook Air. It had a lighter and thinner chassis. The MacBook Pro with a touch bar was priced at $2399, while the one without was going for $1499.

The touch-bar MacBook Pro was more advanced than the one without. The touch bar adapted dynamically to each active application and replaced the row of traditional function keys. A Touch ID sensor was built into the touch bar. The new MacBook Pro featured Thunderbolt 3 or USB-C ports, a second-generation butterfly mechanism keyboard and trackpad, and a brighter, wider gamut display. Other changes to the MacBook Pro included improved speakers with a higher dynamic range, a significantly faster PCIe-based solid-state drive, and a new color, space gray.

The MacBook Pro features a consistent, slab-style design. It also has ventilation and fans. This laptop is faster than the MacBook Air, allowing it to perform harder and longer, with improved overall performance. The ability of the MacBook Pro to run at higher temperatures enables its high performance. Its active cooling system efficiently keeps the systems cool.

Although the performance difference is not significant, it is preferable to use a MacBook Pro if you prefer improved performance. The MacBook Pro includes a standard 8-core GPU (Newsroom, 2020). The MacBook Pro is the best choice for a lot of graphics-intensive work. It is only $50 more expensive than the MacBook Air's 8-core GPU model.

The 13.3-inch backlit display on the MacBook Pro features IPS technology, P3 wide color, and true tone. All of these features are shared by the MacBook Air. As a result, the colors and content will be similar on both devices. The MacBook Pro, on the other hand, has a maximum brightness of 500 nits. This indicates that the MacBook can be 20 percent brighter. If you prefer a brighter display, the MacBook Pro is the way to go.

The battery life of the MacBook Pro is up to 20 hours. As previously stated, the MacBook Pro has a consistent, slab-style design and can accommodate larger batteries. This contributes to the extended battery life.

The MacBook Air has a three-microphone array with directional beamforming, which is studio-quality. It also has stereo speakers with a high dynamic range. Consider using the MacBook Pro for heavy video content consumption or to listen to music through the built-in speakers.

It includes a touch bar. The touch bar has a multi-touch display with "Retina quality." The touch bar's controls change depending on the application you're using, which is an intriguing feature. For example, the touch bar makes it easy to access emojis in Messages and provides a quick way to scroll through videos or edit images. Safari's touch bar can display Favorites and Tabs.

CHAPTER 3

BASIC TERMINOLOGY ABOUT MAIN FUNCTIONS

Software

Asoftware is a set of instructions that instructs a computer or laptop on how to perform a specific task. Application and system software are the two main types of softwares. Application software is software that is installed on a computer system to allow the user to perform a specific task. A browser, for example, allows you to view internet pages, whereas a word processor allows you to type a document. Spreadsheets, database management, email programs, media players, translation, and desktop publishing are other examples of application software.

The system software aids in the administration and operation of a computer or laptop. The system software serves as a bridge between application software, hardware, and the user. Among the many functions of the system software are storage space management, resource allocation, security, and file retrieval. Device drivers, operating systems, utilities, and programming software are the most important types of system software to understand.

The operating system coordinates and controls the hardware, software, and applications on the computer. A laptop or computer cannot function without an operating system. The operating system starts the computer, manages files and resources, and handles input and output. Apple iOS, macOS, Linux, and Android OS are examples of operating systems.

A utility software program is one that aids in the setup, configuration, analysis, strengthening, and maintenance of a computer. Utility software serves a specific purpose. It serves as a backup program, screen saver, memory tester, and antivirus.

Another important type of system software is the device driver, which controls specific hardware connected to the computer. The primary function of a device driver is to act as a translator between the hardware and the operating systems or other applications that use it. It instructs the computer on how to communicate with the device by translating the operating system's set of instructions into a language that the device understands. At the end of the day, the device can complete the task. USB, motherboard, display, and sound card drivers are examples of device drivers.

Hardware

Hardware comprises the computer's physical components. Hardware is further classified into two types: internal hardware and external hardware. External hardware devices are those that are physically separate from the computer. Input and output devices are two types of external hardware. An input device facilitates the process of entering data into a computer or laptop for processing. Output devices receive data from the computer and process it to produce the desired result. The mouse, keyboard, touchpad, microphone, webcam, speaker, screen, and headphones are all examples of external hardware. The CPU and RAM are examples of internal hardware devices found inside a computer or laptop.

App

The full word for 'app' is 'application'. Apple gives this name to programs that you install on Mac OS X and iOS devices for various functions and uses. However, some programs are pre-installed and therefore cannot be deleted.

MacOS And Its Update

The operating system of Macbooks is called macOS. All new Macs have the latest version of Apple's advanced operating system called macOS Big Sur. Big Sur features a wonderful redesign that is completely new but instantly familiar. It also offers powerful updates to applications such as Maps, Messaging, and Safari. Big Sur is remarkable because it has been revamped to enable it to utilize the M1 chip's power.

App Store

An App Store is a digital store where Apple sells Mac OS X and iOS applications. It can also refer to Apple programs on each platform that allow you to access the stores. Once you have access, you can purchase, pay for, and download applications.

Apple Music

Apple Music, a streaming service, allows you to listen to over 90 million songs. You can use this service to download tracks that you like and then play them offline if you want. In addition to listening to original and exclusive music, you can get lyrics in real time and listen on your preferred devices.

The Apple ID

An Apple ID is a user account that can be used to make Apple Store purchases. Apple IDs can also be used to sign up for other Apple services like Find My iPhone and iCloud. To create an Apple ID, go to Settings, then iCloud in iOS and Settings. Then, on Mac OS X, navigate to iCloud.

iCloud

This refers to a variety of services provided by Apple. Calendar sync, push email, and iTunes Match are some of the outstanding features of iCloud. Your iCloud data is available on the go.

GB

GB is an abbreviation for 'gigabyte,' which is a data storage measurement used by smartphones, tablets, computers, gaming consoles, and other computing devices. A gigabyte is made up of 1024 megabytes. A gigabyte can store 3000 ebooks or between 5000 and 15000 documents, depending on size.

Settings

The Settings app comes pre-installed and allows you to customize many aspects of your device's system. This may include turning on or off data roaming or Wi-Fi, changing the desktop wallpaper, or configuring specific settings for other applications. The Settings application icon resembles a slew of gray gears. This application is very useful because it allows you to customize certain aspects of your computer, making it more enjoyable to use.

Gestures

These are a set of movements done by fingers in order to interact with touch screen devices. Common gestures include 'flick', tap, pinch, and unpinch. The flick gesture is characterized by swiftly moving your finger in a downward or upward manner. It is usually used when you want to scroll up or down a web page. It's sometimes used when you want to move through a long list of items.

The tap gesture is the same as clicking with your finger. Another gesture, the pinch, is the movement of the pinching finger and the thumb. This is usually used when you want to zoom in on items. Lastly, the unpinch gesture is the opposite of the pinch. This gesture is used for zooming out.

Lightning

Apple gives this name to the connection port on its laptops, desktops, or phones. The connection port is used to connect to the mains for charging. It can also be connected to other computers for syncing and charging purposes.

Cellular

Cellular is a network technology that enables mobile device communication over areas that have transceivers and cells. The transceivers and cells are also known as cell sites or base stations. In a cellular network, commonly used mobile transceivers are cell phones or mobile phones. Cellular technology enables mobile device users to carry out a number of tasks such as message transmission, placing calls, Facebook updates, and Web browsing.

Desktop

A desktop is commonly used to refer to a system unit. However, the graphical user interface or operating system mainly refers to the way icons are organized on a screen. In this sense, the desktop shows icons for your Internet browser, Recycle Bin, and Task Bar, just to mention a few.

4k

It is named after the number 4000, which refers to 4000 horizontal pixels. This is a new monitor and television that will likely replace high-definition technology. The most common has a 3840x2160 pixel resolution, which is four times that of a high-definition television set. It is possible to edit a 4K video on a Mac Pro, which would be extremely difficult on other laptops that have not been updated to this level.

3D Touch

This is a new touchscreen technology introduced by Apple with the release of the iPhone 6s and 6s Plus. The term "3D touch" refers to sensitivity caused by different amounts of pressure that can be applied to a device. Simply put, depending on how hard you press, different functions on your Apple device may be activated. Apple 3D touch allows you to swipe or push on the screen with more force to preview different types of content. You could also access application functions directly from the home screen.

CPU (Central Processing Unit)

It is in charge of processing all instructions sent by the computer's hardware and software. The CPU is also known as a processor, central processor, or microprocessor. Although the CPU is commonly referred to as the computer's brain, it is more appropriate to refer to software as the brain and the CPU as the efficient calculator. This is due to the CPU's exceptional numerical abilities. However, without the software, the CPU would be unable to perform any other functions. The arithmetic logic unit (ALU) and control unit (CU) are the two main components of the CPU. The ALU performs logical, mathematical, and decision-making operations, whereas the CU directs all processor operations.

GPU

GPU is an abbreviation for graphics processing unit. The GPU is critical for both commercial and personal computing. Despite their popularity in gaming, GPUs have numerous applications in artificial intelligence and creative production.

Originally, GPUs were intended to accelerate 3D graphics projection. However, as time went on, GPUs became more programmable and flexible, enhancing their capabilities. The enhanced capabilities of GPUs enabled the development of more exciting visual effects and realistic acts with shadowing techniques and advanced lighting. Other developers began to use GPU power to increase workloads in high-performance computing and other areas. GPUs are currently used in gaming, machine learning, video editing, and content creation.

RAM

Random-access memory (RAM) is computer hardware that allows for the storage and retrieval of data. RAM is also referred to as primary, system, or main memory. Data in RAM is accessed quickly and haphazardly rather than sequentially. RAM is made up of volatile memory. As a result, power is required to keep the data accessible. When a computer is turned off, all of the RAM data is lost.

The amount of memory available to a computer determines its performance primarily. If a computer does not have enough memory to run the operating system and its programs, performance suffers. A computer with more memory can load more information and software, allowing it to process information at a faster rate.

IPS Technology

IPS stands for in-plane switching. It is a type of monitor that provides improved color reproduction. Apple MacBooks, iPhone, iPod touch models, and iPads use IPS displays. This explains the incomparable color projection of these devices.

CHAPTER 4

HOW TO SETUP YOUR MACBOOK FOR THE FIRST TIME

If you just got the new MacBook Pro, congrats on this awesome journey. You'll need to set up your device to use it effectively for whatever purpose you desire. Here you'll find the step-by-step guidelines to set up and start using your Mac.

First, power on your Mac by pressing the Power button.

Choose a language. The text on your Mac will be written in this language.

Tap Continue.

Next, choose a keyboard layout.

Tap Continue.

Then, choose your Wi-Fi network.

However, if your connection is via Ethernet, choose **Other Network Options**. From there, choose **Ethernet**.

Proceed by inputting your Wi-Fi password if you decide to use Wi-Fi.

Tap Continue.

This could take a few moments. The caption "Looking for networks" will display with a rotating wheel. This is entirely typical.

To set up the Mac as a new device, choose **Don't transfer any information now**.

Now, tap **Continue**.

Then, checkmark the option with the caption **"Enable Location Services on this Mac."**

This allows Apple access to your location and is used to offer improved services for Maps, Siri, etc. If you don't want this, then don't checkmark the box.

Tap Continue.

From there, log in using your Apple ID. Ensure you're using the same Apple ID enrolled on your other Apple devices to allow sync services between the devices. However, if you do not have an Apple ID right now, you can create it later on your Mac.

So, if you've got two-factor authentication activated, you'll be prompted to confirm your identity.

Now, tap **Continue**.

Review every section of the terms and conditions page by tapping **More**, and then choose **Agree** to indicate your approval of these terms.

If asked again, tap **Agree**.

Continue by giving your Mac a name. If you're already logged in with your Apple ID, it will fill up automatically.

After that, enter an Account name. It will also fill up automatically if you are already logged in with your Apple ID.

Then, to secure your computer, enter a password. This is the password you'll use to create new accounts and access system features on your computer.

Following that, enter a Hint to help you remember your password. When you enter an incorrect password, the hint will appear on your Mac Lock screen.

Then, check the box next to "Allow my Apple ID to reset this password." If you have forgotten or lost your Apple ID and password, you can reset your account using this method.

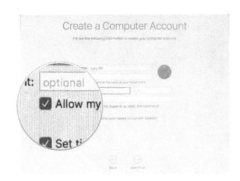 

Then, checkmark the option **"Set time zone based on current location."** However, it'll only work if you turned on **Location Services** as previously advised.

Your date and time will be automatically updated when you go to new locations outside of your current time zone if this option is set.

Tap **Continue**. At this moment, iCloud will start to sync if you're already logged in.

Then, checkmark the option **"Turn on FileVault disk encryption."** This feature encrypts the documents on your computer hard drive.

 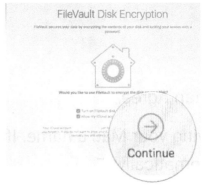

Follow up by ticking the option to **"Allow my iCloud account to unlock my disk."** This feature can also be used to reset your device password.

From there, tap **Continue**.

Then, checkmark the option **"Store files from Documents and Desktop in iCloud."** You should only checkmark this option if you have sufficient iCloud storage that can contain your entire Desktop and Documents files and directories to sync.

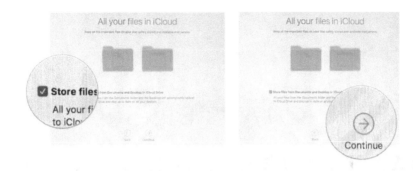

Tap Continue.

Next, checkmark the option **"Enable Siri on this Mac."** Siri is a personal voice assistant for all Apple devices.

Tap Continue.

Afterward, your Mac will begin to complete all settings and syncing. The caption "S**etting up**" may appear on the screen.

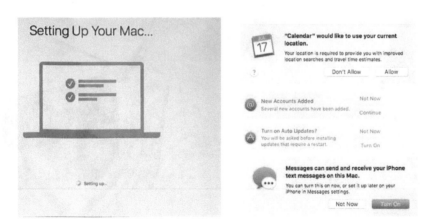

Once the setup is complete, you'd get a pop-up notice to log into different mail and social accounts. Follow up by tapping **Allow**, or **Turn On** for the respective notification to log in.

CHAPTER 5

HOW TO ORGANIZE FILES, USE FINDER, ACCESS ICLOUD, BACKUP YOUR FILES & MORE

Hide Recent Apps

You can decongest the Dock of your Mac computer by taking away a recently opened application. This makes your device look tidy and not cramped up.

- From your MacBook Pro, tap the Apple icon at the upper-left corner.
- **Next, tap** System Preferences.
- **Then, tap** Dock & Menu Bar.
- Proceed by tapping the box beside the **Show recent applications** in the Dock option.

- After you've checkmark the box, that additional section in the Dock will go away. So, you'll be left with only the applications that you need.

Change Position Of Dock

There are two methods to conveniently adjust the position of the Dock on your computer. Let's begin with the first one.

Method 1:

- Begin by right-clicking on the separator between your applications and downloads.
- Using your Mac's pointer, tap **Position on the screen**.

- Proceed by choosing between Right, Left, or Bottom.

Method 2: In the upper-left corner of your MacBook Pro, tap the Apple icon.

Then, select System Preferences.

Then, select Dock & Menu Bar.

Then, next to the Position on-screen option, select Right, Left, or Bottom.

If you move the Dock to the left or right, you will lose some screen space in the width area, but you will be able to view more pages vertically. As a result, most users prefer to use the dock in one of the two locations rather than the bottom to see more of the page.

Magnification can be changed using the following steps:

You can enlarge apps in the Mac's Dock by hovering your cursor over them. You can shrink the dock in this manner while still being able to click and launch the necessary applications whenever necessary.

Tap the Apple icon in the upper-left corner of your MacBook Pro.

Then, select System Preferences.

Then, select Dock & Menu Bar.

Then, check the box next to the Magnification option.

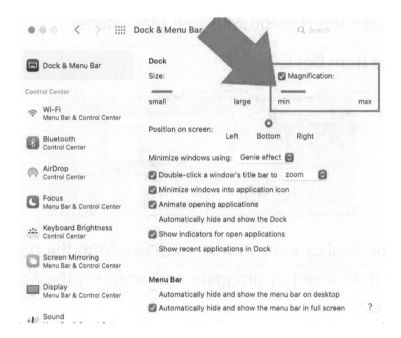

- Proceed by adjusting the slider as required.
- Whenever you wish to use Magnification on your Mac's Dock, ensure that the slider is much higher than the **"Size"**. It'll guarantee that the icons will definitely magnify whenever the pointer floats across them in the Dock.

Add Or Remove Apps From Dock

Adding and removing applications from the Dock is a critical component of personalizing the Dock. When you close all of your other apps, only the apps you use the most will be displayed.

To begin, launch Launchpad from your Mac's Dock.

Locate the application that you want to include in the Dock.

Finish by dragging and dropping the app into the desired location on the Dock.

So, if you want an app to stay on the Dock, right-click it and select Options. Tap Keep in Dock from there.

To remove apps from the Dock, follow these steps:

Locate the application that you want to remove from Dock.

Then, right-click on the application and select Properties.

Tap Options from the context menu with your Mac pointer.

Then select Remove from Dock.

- However, if the application you wish to delete from the Dock is already open, tap and hold it. Proceed by dragging and dropping the application off of the Dock to delete it.

Add Folders To Dock

You can conveniently add your favorite folders/directories to the Dock for easy usage by following the guideline below.

- From your MacBook Pro, launch the Finder application.
- Proceed by moving to the folder you desire to add to the Dock.
- Follow up by right-clicking the folder.
- From the context menu, tap **Add to Dock**.

- Note: not every folder can be added to Dock. However, most of them in the Finder's sidebar can be added.

Automatically Hide And Show Dock

When you're not using your MacBook Pro, you can set it to automatically hide the Dock, giving you more desktop space.

Tap the Apple icon in the upper-left corner of your MacBook Pro.

- Next, select System Preferences.
- Next, select Dock & Menu Bar.
- Next, check the box next to the option to automatically hide and show the Dock.

Resize The Dock

You can expand or shrink the icon that appears on the Dock as well as adjust their real size by following the guidelines below.

Method 1:

- Launch the System Preferences application.
- **Then, tap** Dock & Menu Bar.
- Below the **Size** section, proceed by adjusting the slider to your desired Dock size.

Method 2:

- Start by floating your Mac's pointer on the vertical separator between docked applications and the Downloads folder.
- As soon as your Mac's pointer changes to an up-and-down arrow, then proceed by clicking and dragging towards the top of the page.

Then, let go if you've achieved your ideal Dock size.

The Finder

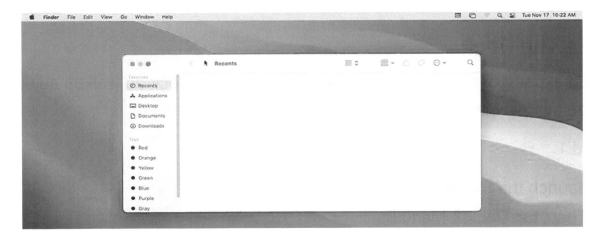

The Finder is the file management tool for the Mac operating system. It is where you can access all the files and folders on your MacBook. On the Finder menu, you can access your Applications, Desktop, Documents, Download, and lots more.

Using The Finder

To open Finder, click on the **Smiley icon** on your Dock, and this will open the Finder window.

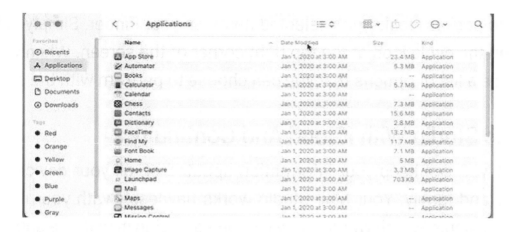

On the window, you will see a series of options on the left side of the window. You will see Airdrop, Recents, Desktop, Documents, and others. You will also see the size of the files, the kind of files, and the date they were modified.

When you click on one of them, the contents of that folder are displayed. For example, if you click on Application, it will show you all of the applications that are currently installed on your computer. When you click Documents, it will show you all of the documents on your computer. When you click on Desktop, the files and folders on your Desktop will be displayed. You can also use the Search icon on the right side of the window to look for files.

When you click on any of the folders on the left side of the Finder window, you'll see various options at the top right-hand side that you can use to customize how the Finder looks. Files can also be shared from the Finder. Choose the file you want to share and then click the share icon in the top right-hand corner of the window. Then, choose where you want to share the file: Mail, Messages, Notes, or More for more options.

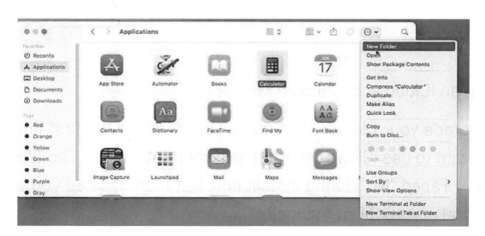

You can also perform tasks with selected items on your Finder. Simply select a file, then click on the circle icon at the top right corner of the screen. When you click on it, you will see a list of options that you can choose to perform with the selected file.

Enjoy Mac Studio With iCloud And Continuity

With iCloud, you can keep your information updated on all your devices and work with friends and family. Your Mac Studio works flawlessly with your iPhone, iPad, iPod touch, or Apple Watch when you use iCloud and sign in with the same Apple ID. You can drag and drop files, share and edit documents, open Mac Studio with Apple Watch, turn your iPhone or iPad into a network, and more.

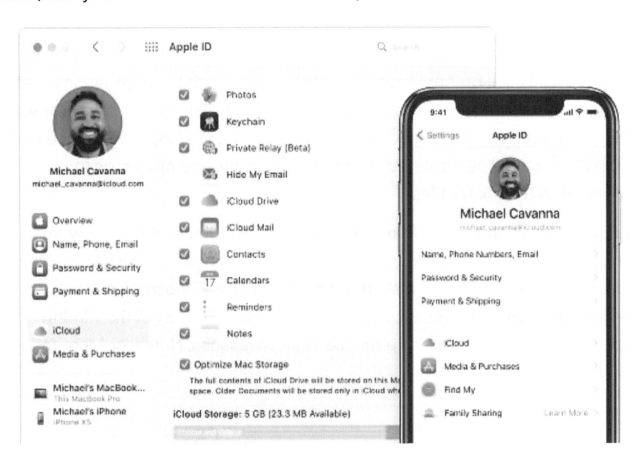

How to set up an iCloud account on a Mac

When you upgrade your Mac or start using your Mac for the first time, you will be asked if you want to use iCloud Drive to store your data. If you Tap "Yes", everything is ready. If you Taped "No" during installation, but then decided you wanted to use iCloud Drive, you can enable it manually.

1. On the top left edge of the screen click on the Apple logo.

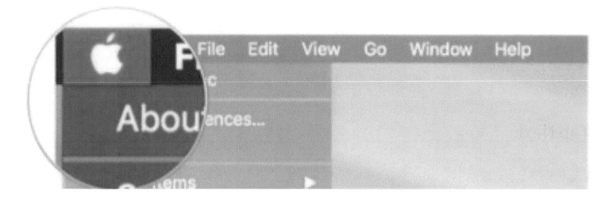

2. Select System Preferences from the drop-down menu.

3. In the upper right corner select 'Sign in'.

4. Type in your Apple ID and password.

5. Tap Next.

6. Select the option Allow to permit Find My Mac in the popup window.

Confirm the boxes next to all iCloud apps.

It would be better if you have control fields for each application; This will cover your settings on all iCloud-enabled devices.

How To Back Up Your Device With Time Machine

1. Connect your hard drive or solid-state drive (alternatively you can use a NAS drive).

2. Your device should prompt you whether you want to use the drive with Time Machine. From the menu, choose Use as Backup Disk.

3. If you do not see the alert, go to System Preferences > Time Machine and select Backup Disk.

4. Choose the storage device and press the Use Disk button.

CHAPTER 6

INTERNET SETUP, SAFARI/CHROME CONFIGURATION, AND APPS

Internet Setup

Take advantage of Wi-Fi

I f a Wi-Fi network is available, the Wi-Fi icon appears in the computer's top menu bar. To connect to a network, first click on the icon, then select one. A lock symbol appears next to the network name in this case, indicating that the network is password-protected; in this case, you must enter the password before connecting to the Wi-Fi network.

Utilize Ethernet

Networking can be accomplished via an Ethernet network or by using a DSL or cable modem. Connect it to your Mac's Ethernet port, which is denoted by an asterisk, using a network cable. If your Mac does not have an Ethernet port built-in, you can connect the Ethernet cable to a USB or Thunderbolt port on your computer by using an adapter. The process of connecting to an Ethernet network is thoroughly explained.

Utilize an instant hotspot

If you don't have access to Wi-Fi or Ethernet at your location, you may be able to connect to the internet using your Mac and Instant Hotspot and your iPhone or iPad's hotspot.

Depending on your location, your internet service provider may provide a Wi-Fi or Ethernet connection when you're at home. If you are unsure about your Internet access, you should contact your Internet service provider.

If you have Wi-Fi or an Ethernet network connection at work, your company's information technology departments or network administrators can provide specifications for connecting to and using the network, as well as information on network usage guidelines.

Safari

How To Begin Using Safari On A Mac

Is it correct that you're having trouble getting started with Safari? This is how you do it!

Safari is Apple's web browser, and it is your primary internet connection. It allows you to browse websites, bookmark favorite pages, and much more. The steps outlined below will assist you in getting started with Safari on your Mac.

How to Use a Website's Navigation Bar

Safari's primary function as a gateway to the internet's millions of websites is to serve as a search engine. You can manually enter the web address, also known as the "URL," of the website you want to visit if you know it.

Depending on your preferences, Safari can be launched from the Dock or the Finder.

Go to the top of the window and click the address bar to access it.

In the box provided, type the website address you want to visit.

On your keyboard, press the Return key.

How to Search Using Your Computer's Browser's Address Bar

You enter the URL into the address bar when you visit a website. However, it is not limited to web addresses; you can also use it to search Google!

Go to the top of the window and click the address bar to access it.

Enter a search term into the search box, such as "funny cat videos."

Your browser will take you to Google, where a list of search results will be displayed.

How to Save a Website to Your Computer as a Bookmark

If you like what you're reading online or need quick access to your favorite websites, you can bookmark them and return to them later with a single click!

Navigate to the website you want to bookmark and enter the required information.

The shortcut key on your keyboard is Command-D.

You can choose to give the bookmark a title or leave it blank if you prefer. You may also provide a synopsis of your argument.

Insert a return key into your keyboard or press the enter key.

There is a menu bar in the upper left corner of your screen with the options View.

From the drop-down menu, select the Show Favorites Bar check box.

All of your Favorites pages will now be accessible with a single click because they will appear below the address bar, making it simple to access them all. Furthermore, your Favorites will appear as suggested sites whenever you click in the address bar.

How to See All of Your Bookmarks at Once

If you don't like having your favorites displayed beneath the address bar, or if you prefer to organize your bookmarks by folder, you can view all of your bookmarks at once.

Choose Show sidebar, which is located next to the address bar.

Select the bookmarks tab from the drop-down menu if it is not already selected. It has a book-like appearance to it.

How to Turn On Private Browsing

Browse the internet anonymously, with no record of the pages you've visited, your search history, or your AutoFill information. You can use it to shop for Christmas gifts or browse the internet for... well, you get the idea.

The file can be found in your computer's top-left menu bar.

From the drop-down menu, choose Create a New Private Window. To achieve the same result, use the keyboard shortcut shift-command-N.

All websites you visit will no longer be saved, and neither will your AutoFill information, ensuring that no one can track your activities through your history.

How to Create a Homepage for Your Website

When you launch Safari, it will navigate to apple.com as the default landing page. It is entirely possible to have a separate website displayed on your homepage.

Enter the URL of a website in the box next to the Homepage. You can also choose Set to Current Page to make the current page the browser's default starting point.

From the drop-down menu next to the phrase "New windows open using," choose the method for opening new windows.

Select Homepage from the drop-down menu if you want new windows to open on your homepage.

Choose New tabs open from the dropdown menu.

Select Homepage from the drop-down menu to open new tabs on your homepage.

CHAPTER 7

SYSTEM PREFERENCES

The System Preferences on your MacBook is the main menu where you get to see all your Mac Settings options. It is how you control settings on your Mac. The System Preferences are located in the Dock by default. It is always available when you click on the Apple Logo at the top left-hand side of your screen, then select System Preferences.

It displays preference categories based on Icon. When you select a category, a menu called Pane, as in Window Pane, appears. You will see your name and information that applies to you as the owner and user of this Mac account at the top of the System Preferences menu. The Apple ID System Preferences will also be visible. When you click, you will be taken to the settings for your Apple ID, iCloud, and other Apple services.

Another thing you can do on the System Preferences menu is Search using the search box at the top right-hand side of the menu.

You can search for an option within a setting rather than just the name of the individual system preferences. For example, the Default web browser setting can be found within the General category icon in the System Preference menu.

You can easily search for the Default web browser on the search box instead of clicking on the General category icon on the System Preference menu.

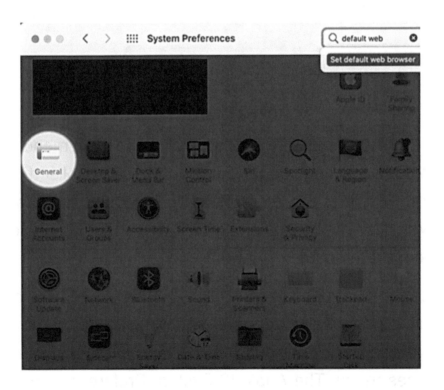

As you can see in the image below, it will show you where the Default web browser option is located, that is in the General option. You can click one of them to open it.

Customizing The System Preferences

You can change the appearance of your System Preferences in different ways. So without further ado, let's show you how you can customize it.

1. Open the menu for the **System Preference**.
2. On top of the screen, click **View**. On the View menu, you can change the organization method of the System Preferences menu. It is organized by **Categories** by default, you can choose to organize it **Alphabetically**.

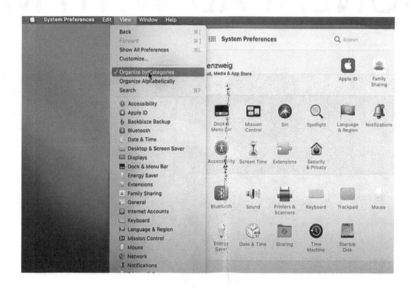

3. You can also hide unwanted preferences panes. On the View menu, select **Customize**.
4. You can turn off the Preference pane by **unchecking** it. Then, click the **Done** button.

CHAPTER 8

HOW TO SETUP YOUR IPHONE/IPAD WITH MAC

It is entirely possible to sync your Macbook data with other Apple devices that you may own, such as the iPhone or the iPad. This can be done mainly through the iTunes application. But even with the absence of iTunes, you can still sync your mobile devices with your Mac computer.

Instead of using iTunes to sync your mobile device, you will now use Finder on your Mac.

Click the Finder app from your Dock.

On the left side of your screen, click on the name of your device.

When you click on this, you will see the interface that you are used to from macOS Mojave.

Backups can now be managed, your device can be restored, and content can be synced between your mobile device and your computer.

Sync Movies Between Your Mac and iPad/iPhone

Click the Finder app from your Dock.

On the left side of your screen, click on the name of your device.

Select the Movies tab.

Tick the box next to Movie Sync to enable it. Sync your movies to your device.

Check the box for Automatically include under sync options.

Choose All from the pull-down menu to select all content or select specific options from the list.

Select Apply.

Then, at the right bottom of the screen, click Sync to sync your movies between your mobile device and the Mac.

Using Mac, Sync Music To Your iPad Or iPhone

If you use iCloud Music library sync on your iPad or iPhone, you cannot sync music to your Mac.

Click the Finder app from your Dock.

On the left side of your screen, click on the name of your device.

Select the Music tab.

Tick the box next to Sync Music onto your device to enable music syncing.

You can sync either "selected playlists, artists, albums, and genres" or "entire music library" under sync options.

Go to Options and, if desired, check the boxes next to "Automatically fill free space with songs" and "Include Videos."

Then, if applicable, select playlists, albums, artists, and genre.

Select Apply.

Then, at the right bottom of the screen, click Sync to sync your music files between your mobile device and the Mac.

Sync Books From Your Mac To Your iPad Or iPhone

Click the Finder app from your Dock.

On the left side of your screen, click on the name of your device.

Select the Books tab.

Tick the box next to Sync Books onto your device to enable Books syncing.

You can select specific books or all the books under the sync option.

If you selected Selected Books, check the boxes next to the books you want to sync.

Select Apply.

Then, at the right bottom of the screen, click Sync to sync your books between your mobile device and the Mac.

Sync Files To Your iPad Or iPhone

Click the Finder app from your Dock.

On the left side of your screen, click on the name of your device.

Select the Files tab.

Tick the box next to Sync Files onto your device to enable Files syncing.

Select either selected files or all files under the sync option.

If you selected Selected files, then check the boxes next to the files you want to sync.

Select Apply.

Then, at the right bottom of the screen, click Sync to sync your books between your mobile device and the Mac.

Sync Photos From Your Mac To Your iPad Or iPhone

If you use the iCloud Photo library sync on your iPad or iPhone, you will be unable to sync photos with your computer.

Click the Finder app from your Dock.

On the left side of your screen, click on the name of your device.

Select the Photos tab.

Select the files you want to sync.

Select Apply.

Then, at the right bottom of the screen, click Sync to sync your photos between your mobile device and the Mac.

MacOS Backup Your iPad Or iPhone

To manually back up your mobile device on your computer, follow the steps below:

Click the Finder app from your Dock.

On the left side of your screen, click on the name of your device.

Select the General tab.

Then, beside the Backup and Restore option, click on Back Up Now.

On Mac, Restore Your iPad Or iPhone.

Follow the steps below to manually restore your mobile device on your computer.

Click the Finder app from your Dock.

On the left side of your screen, click on the name of your device.

Select the General tab.

Then, beside the Backup and Restore option, click on Restore Back-Up.

CHAPTER 9
PRODUCTIVITY APPS

Calendar

The Calendar ensures that your appointments and events are never missed. Create multiple calendars and manage them from a single location to keep track of your busy schedule.

Create occasions. Double-click ✛ anywhere on the calendar to add a new event. To invite someone to an event, double-click the event, then click the Add Invitees section and enter their email address. The Calendar notifies you of invitation responses.

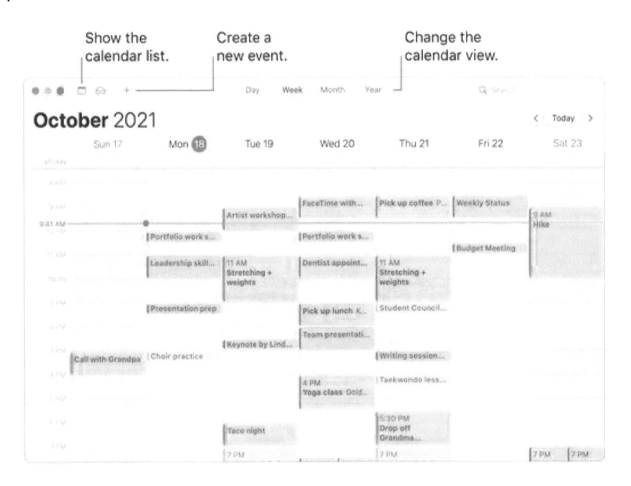

When you add a location to an event, the Calendar displays a map, estimated travel time and departure time, as well as the weather forecast.

A calendar for all aspects of life: Create distinct, color-coded calendars, for example, for home, work, and school. To create a new calendar, select File > New Calendar, then Control-click each calendar to change its color.

View all of your Calendars or just a few of them. Click the Calendars button to see a list of your calendars; then, in the window, click the calendars you want to see.

Share data among your devices and with others. When you sign in to iCloud, your calendars are synchronized across all of your Macs, iOS devices, iPadOS devices, and Apple Watches that use the same Apple ID. Calendars can also be shared with other iCloud users.

Photos

Use Photos and iCloud Photos to organize, edit, and share photos and videos, as well as to keep your photo library up to date across all of your devices. Photos displays your best photos, and with improved search capabilities, it's simple to find and enjoy your favorites. With the help of simple editing tools, you can edit your photos and videos like a pro.

Automatically create
a personalized video
of special moments.

View your photos by
Years, Months, Days,
or All Photos.

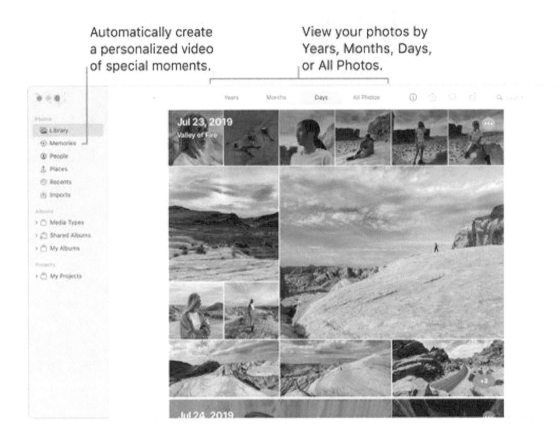

All of your photos on all of your devices: iCloud Photos allows you to view, search, and share photos and videos stored on all of your Apple ID-authenticated devices. When you take a picture with your iPhone, it syncs with all of your other devices. And any changes you make to your photos are reflected on all of your devices. To begin, open System Preferences, then select Apple ID, iCloud, and Photos.

Access photos shared by your friends: When friends in your Contacts send you photos via Messages, they appear in your Photos app's Shared with You section. Photos from events you attended that you are likely to remember are saved in your library. By tapping the message bubble on a photo while viewing photos in the Photos app, you can open Messages and continue a conversation.

Edit like a professional: You can make photos and videos that stand out by using powerful but simple editing tools. To quickly improve your photo or video, use the editing tools above it. To achieve professional results, click Edit to access more powerful editing tools, then use Smart Sliders. Cropping, filtering, rotating, and increasing the exposure of photos and videos are some of the options.

Play with the text: Live Text recognizes text contained within images on your computer and the Internet. On a Mac, you can copy text from an image and paste it into any file, or you can click a phone number or website to call or open it. Select the text to be translated, right-click it with Control, and then click Translate.

Relive important moments: Photos commemorate important events such as birthdays, anniversaries, and vacations. As you scroll through your photo library, Live Photos and videos begin to play. When you click Memories in the sidebar, Photos will create a personalized, shareable video with music, titles, moods, and transitions. All of your other iCloud Photos-enabled devices can access your Memories.

Find what you're looking for: Photos focuses on the best images in your collection while hiding duplicates, receipts, and screenshots. To view photos by year, month, or day, use the buttons at the top of the Photos window; alternatively, click All Photos to see the entire collection. Photos recognizes objects, scenes, and people in your photos and videos, allowing you to search them based on what's in them, the date they were taken, the people you've named in them, the captions you've added, and their location if provided. You can also use the spotlight and Siri to search for photos.

People, places, and things: Visual Lookup recognizes a variety of objects in your photographs. To highlight objects and scenes that have been identified, swipe up on a photo or click the information button on a photo. Discover more about well-known world art and landmarks, plants and flowers, books, and pet breeds. To keep important people's photos at the top of the People album, click the Favorites button next to their image. View all of your geotagged photos on an interactive map by using the Places album. Zoom in on the map to see more images from a specific location.

Add location to any photograph: Click the Information button while viewing the image, then select Assign Location and start typing. Select a location from the drop-down menu, or enter it manually and press Return.

With Live Photos, you can let your imagination run wild: With Live Photos, use the Loop effect to loop the action indefinitely, and the Bounce effect to play the animation forward and backward. For a professional DSLR look, use Long Exposure to blur motion in your Live Photos and turn an ordinary waterfall or stream into a work of art.

Facetime

FaceTime allows you to make video and audio calls to a friend or group of friends from your Mac.

Ask Siri: Say something like, "Call Sharon via FaceTime."

FaceTime call made: Utilize the FaceTime HD camera built into your Mac to conduct FaceTime video calls. Click New FaceTime, enter the person's name, phone number, or email address, and then click FaceTime. If it is not convenient to make a video call, select FaceTime Audio from the pop-up menu to make an audio-only call. When you receive a FaceTime invitation, you have the option of joining with video or audio-only.

You can drag the small picture-in-picture window to any corner of the FaceTime window while a video call is active.

List of recent calls

Utilize FaceTime as a group: In a group call, you can connect with up to 32 people. Create a link to share with the group. Click Link Creation. Copy the link to the Clipboard or send it directly to friends through Messages or Email. Non-Apple devices can now join FaceTime calls via a link.

Add a FaceTime link to a Calendar event to schedule a future call.

Recognition of sign language and Live Captions: FaceTime detects when a participant in a Group FaceTime call is using sign language and highlights that individual. FaceTime Live Captions recognize speech and display real-time captions for the active speaker.

Make a Call. If you have an iPhone with iOS 8 or later, you can use FaceTime to make phone calls from your Mac. Just ensure that your Mac and iPhone are signed in with the same Apple ID and that the feature is enabled on both devices. Open FaceTime on your Mac, navigate to FaceTime > Preferences, and then select "Calls from iPhone."

Note: To make or receive calls on your Mac, your MacBook Pro and iPhone must be connected to the internet and on the same Wi-Fi network.

Music

The Music app facilitates the organization and enjoyment of your iTunes Store purchases, songs, and albums in your library, as well as the Apple Music catalog (which lets you listen to millions of songs on demand). Click to view the next track, previously played tracks, and lyrics for the current track. The iTunes Store is a place to purchase music.

It is located in your library: You can easily view and play your iTunes Store purchases, Music catalog additions, and music in your library. You can filter content by Recently Added, Artists, Albums, and Songs.

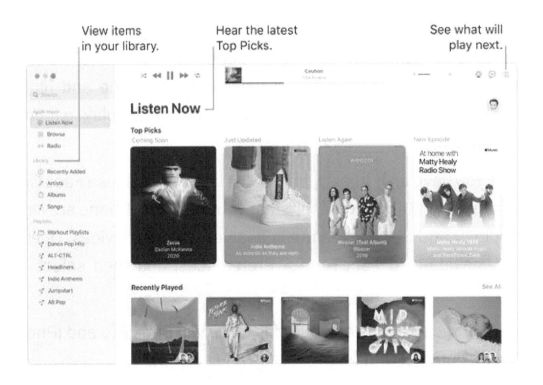

Explore the highlights of Apple Music: Click Browse in the sidebar to view new music and exclusive releases from Apple Music, a monthly fee-based music streaming service. Stream and download more than 50 million songs without ads, and choose from a wide variety of playlists to find the perfect mix for any occasion.

Sing along: Click 💬 on the toolbar to display a panel with the current song's lyrics (if available).

Tune in: Click Radio in the sidebar to listen to any episode from the Apple Music family of shows or to listen to Apple Music 1 live. Explore the various stations created for nearly every musical genre.

Ask Siri: Include the phrase "Add this song to my library"

Sync effortlessly: Sync your music directly within the Apple Music application. When you connect a device, it appears in the Finder's sidebar. Simply drag the desired content onto your device. In the Finder, you can also back up and restore your device.

Purchase it via the iTunes Store: To purchase music, select iTunes Store from the sidebar. (If the store is not visible in the sidebar, select Music > Preferences > General, then click Show iTunes Store.)

Tip: When screen space is limited, switch to MiniPlayer to open a small, movable window that allows you to listen to and control your music while performing other tasks on your Mac. Choose Window > MiniPlayer to launch MiniPlayer.

Numbers

Use Numbers on your Mac to create attractive and powerful spreadsheets. More than thirty templates designed by Apple give you a head start on creating budgets, invoices, and other documents. Microsoft Excel spreadsheets can also be opened and exported in Numbers.

Start with a template and add your information: Select the template's sample text, then enter your text. Drag a graphic file from your Mac onto the placeholder image to add images.

Use sheets to organize yourself: Use multiple sheets or tabs to display a variety of data views. Use one sheet for your budget, another for your table, and a third for your notes, for instance. Simply click to add a new sheet. To rearrange sheets, drag a tab to the left or right.

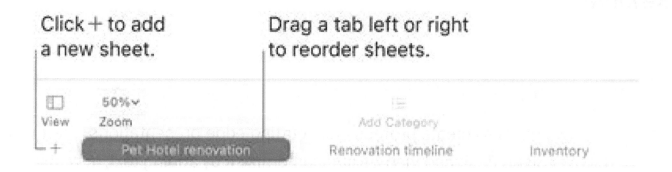

Click + to add a new sheet.

Drag a tab left or right to reorder sheets.

Formulas are easy: Simply type the equal sign (=) in a cell to view a sidebar with a list of all the functions and their descriptions. When you begin to type a formula, instant suggestions will appear.

Select the range of cells containing the values to receive instant calculations for a series of values. You'll find the sum, average, minimum, maximum, and count of the selected values at the bottom of the window. To view additional options, click the Menu button in the bottom-right corner.

Build pivot tables: Create a pivot table using a table or range of cells in a spreadsheet as the source data, and then use it to analyze any data set, quickly group and summarize values, and identify interesting patterns and trends. You can modify the cell range of your source data, add and organize pivot table data, and create a copyable snapshot of a pivot table.

Keynote

Keynote allows users to create professional, cutting-edge presentations. Start with one of the over 30 predesigned themes and customize it by adding text, new objects, and modifying the color scheme.

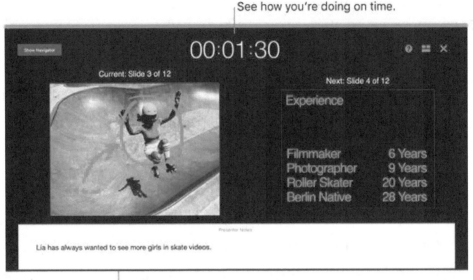

See how you're doing on time.

Remind yourself
of key points to make.

Organize graphically: Utilize the slide navigator on the left to add, rearrange, and delete slides quickly. Select a slide and press Delete to delete it.

Practice leads to mastery: To practice your presentation, select the Play > Rehearse Slideshow menu option. You will see each slide alongside your notes and a timer to help you stay on schedule.

Present in all circumstances: Present using an external display while using your Mac to view upcoming slides, presenter notes, a clock, and a timer. Control a multi-presenter slideshow during a videoconference as you would if you were the only presenter. Create an interactive presentation that is controlled by the audience, or control your presentation remotely with your iPhone, iPad, or even Apple Watch, and more.

Share your presentation with others: If your manager wants to review your presentation or you want to share it on a conference call, select Share > Send a Copy to send a copy via Mail, Messages, AirDrop, or social media.

Draw in: Get their attention by animating a slide's object. Select the object, then click Animate in the toolbar, Action in the sidebar, and Add Effect.

Incorporate a video into your presentation: Click the desired location, then click the Media icon in the toolbar. Click Movies, then locate the desired video and drag it to the slide.

Mail

It allows you to manage all of your email accounts through a single application. It is compatible with the majority of popular email providers, including iCloud, Gmail, Yahoo Mail, and AOL Mail.

One-stop email: Are you sick of logging in to multiple websites to check your email? Configure Mail with all of your accounts so you can view all of your messages in a single location. Select Mail > Create Account.

Ask Siri: Send an email to Laura regarding the trip.

Determine the ideal message: Enter text in the search box to see suggested messages that match your query.

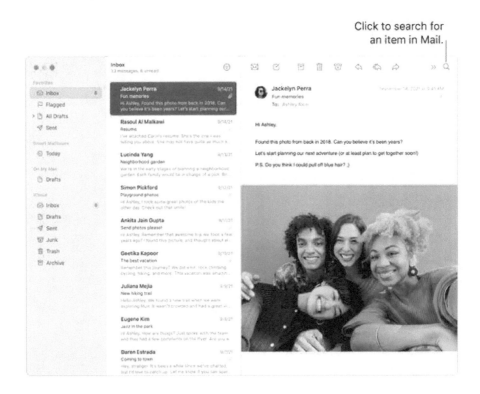

Click to search for an item in Mail.

Concentrate on what is most important: In your inbox, only show the messages you want to see. Within Mail, you can mute excessively active email threads and unsubscribe from mailing lists.

Directly from Mail, add contacts and events: When you receive a message with a new email address or event, click Add in the message to add it to your Contacts or Calendar. When you force-click an address, a map preview appears that you can open in Maps.

Maintain your privacy: Privacy Protection keeps email senders from learning about your Mail activity. It masks your IP address so that senders cannot associate it with your online activity or determine your location if it is enabled. It also prevents senders from knowing if their email has been opened or not. Select Protect Mail Activity in Mail Preferences > Privacy to enable the feature.

Translate in a flash: Choose the text to be translated. Control-click the text, then choose Translate and a language. Select "Replace with Translation" to translate typed text. To download languages for offline use, navigate to the Language & Region section of System Preferences, then click the Translation Languages button at the bottom.

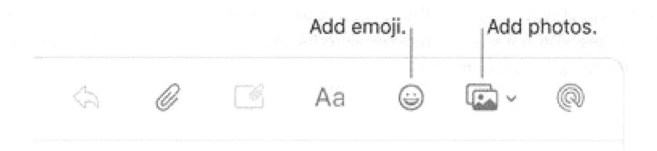

Personalize any message: With a single click, you can add images or emojis. Select images from your photo library or take new ones with your iPhone or iPad. You can also include a drawing you made on your iPhone or iPad.

View on a large screen: When using Mail in full-screen mode, new message windows automatically open in Split View on the right, allowing you to easily refer to another message in your inbox while writing.

Never overlook an email: Check the Mail icon in the Dock to determine how many unread messages you have. When you receive a new email, a notification appears in the upper-right corner of the screen, allowing you to quickly review incoming messages. (Do not wish to receive alerts? Open System Preferences, then click Notifications to disable them.)

Notes

Text is not the only type of note. Fill in the blanks with checklists, images, and hyperlinks, or scribble down quick ideas. Create a Quick Note from any app or website, on the Desktop, in full-screen or Split View mode. Create and use tags to organize your notes and make it easier to find similar notes. You can share an entire folder of notes with a group, allowing everyone to collaborate. Include mentions (@name) in your notes to notify someone of new content that they will find useful. In the Activity view, you can also see all recent changes.

Inquire Siri: Say something along the lines of "Make a new note."

Create a Quick Note from anywhere: You can create a note from any application or website on your Mac and view it at any time in the new Quick Notes sidebar category with the new Quick Notes feature. Without having to open Notes, you can capture your thoughts, remember a location, or link to a website you want to remember, regardless of what you're doing on your Mac. When you return to the original app or website, a thumbnail of your Quick Note appears to remind you of the important information you recorded. To open the Quick Notes app, tap it.

Simple to reach: To create a Quick Note wherever you are, use the Fn-Q keyboard shortcut or a Hot Corner specified in System Preferences > Desktop & Screen Saver. In Safari, you can add text to a note by selecting it and then clicking Share > Add Quick Note.

Add notes, secure them, and share them: Using the Notes toolbar, you can quickly add checklists, images, videos, sketches, tables, and links to your note. Use a passphrase to encrypt your note. Include a copy of the note in Mail, Messages, Reminders, or AirDrop and send it to collaborators.

When you sign in with your Apple ID and enable iCloud Notes, your notes are synchronized across all of your devices, allowing you to make a to-do list on your Mac and then check items off on your iPhone while on the go.

Adding tags: Tags can be used anywhere in the body of your note to organize and categorize its contents. Your tag text should come after the # symbol. To quickly navigate to notes containing a specific tag (such as #vacation or #cooking), you can view your tags in the sidebar. Custom Smart Folders organize similar tags into a single location.

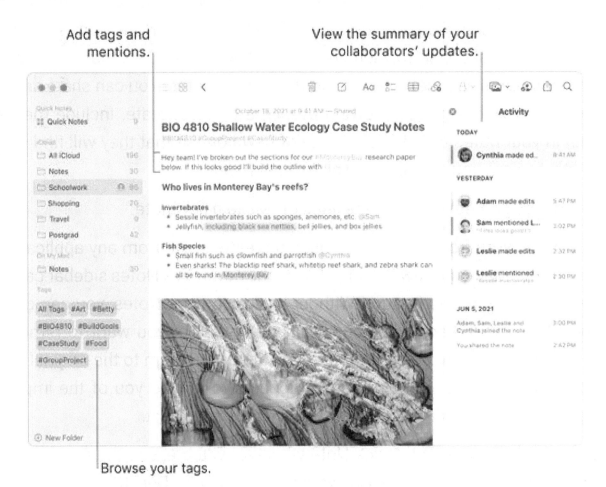

Browse your tags.

Use mentions. **Add mentions (typing @ followed** by a name, such as @Leslie) to connect directly with your project or social collaborators. They will receive a notification when they are mentioned in a note, and they can immediately participate.

View the activity summary of a note: View the most recent updates regarding who has been working on a shared note in the Activity view on the Notes window's right side. Swipe right on the text of a note to view editor callouts highlighting changes and the date and time the note was edited.

Personalize the toolbar: Control-clicking anywhere on the toolbar will launch the Customize Toolbar window. Simply by dragging your preferred items into the toolbar, you can make it useful.

Pages

Create media-rich documents and books on your Mac using the Pages application. Open and edit Microsoft Word documents while keeping track of changes made by yourself and others.

Look good! Pages provides professional, ready-to-use templates for books, newsletters, reports, and resumes, making it simple to begin a project.

All formatting tools in one location: To open the Format inspector, select the Format button in the toolbar. When you select an item in your document, the formatting options for it will appear.

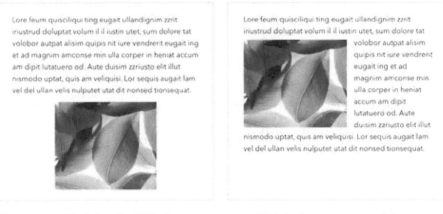

Move a graphic into a text block...   **...and the text wraps around the graphic automatically.**

The text must flow around images: When an image is added to a text document, the text will automatically flow around it. In the Format sidebar, you can adjust the wrapping of text.

Improve your publishing abilities: Pages includes book templates for creating interactive EPUB books. Include a table of contents, as well as text and images. When your book is finished, you can make it available for purchase or download in Apple Books.

Begin on the Mac and end on the iPad: When you sign in with the same Apple ID on all of your devices, you can keep your documents up to date. As a result, you can start writing on one device and continue on another.

Translate quickly: Choose the text to be translated. Control-click it, then choose Translate and a language. To translate typed text, click "Replace with Translation." You can also download languages for offline use by going to System Preferences, Language & Region, and clicking the Translation Languages button at the bottom.

Enable change tracking to see the changes you and others have made to a document: Each person's edits and comments are color-coded, so you can see who made each change. To display the tracking toolbar, go to Edit > Track Changes.

Reminders

Reminder makes it easier than ever to keep track of your responsibilities. Create and organize reminders for grocery lists, work projects, and anything else you wish to monitor. Additionally, you can decide when and where to receive reminders. Create groups to assign shared project tasks.

Add tags: Add tags to your reminders to organize them. Simply click one or more tags in the sidebar to filter reminders quickly.

Create custom intelligent lists: Smart Lists automatically organize upcoming reminders according to dates, times, tags, locations, flags, and priority. Create custom intelligent lists by applying filters.

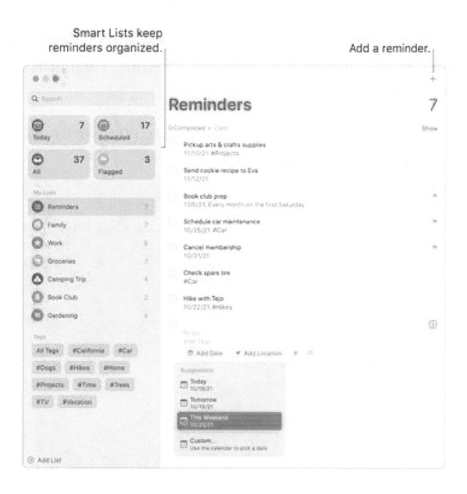

Use smart suggestions: Reminders suggests dates, times, and locations for a reminder based on similar reminders you have previously created.

Assign accountability: Assign reminders to individuals with whom you share a list so that they receive a notification. Distribute tasks and ensure that everyone is aware of their responsibilities. Choose File > Share List to share a list.

Utilize subtasks and groups to organize: To transform a reminder into a subtask, press Command-] or drag it over another reminder. The parent reminder is italicized, while the subtask is indented beneath it. You can collapse or expand subtasks to maintain a clean view.

To group reminders, select File, then New Group. You may give the group any name you like. Add additional lists to the group by dragging them in, or remove them by dragging them out.

Get reminder suggestions in Mail: When corresponding with someone in Mail, Siri can identify potential reminders and provide suggestions for creating them.

Add a quick reminder: Use natural language to add a reminder quickly. To create a recurring reminder for that day and time, you could write "Take Amy to soccer every Wednesday at 5 p.m."

Ask Siri: Say, "Remind me to stop at the grocery store on my way out of here."

CHAPTER 10

MACBOOK ACCESSORIES

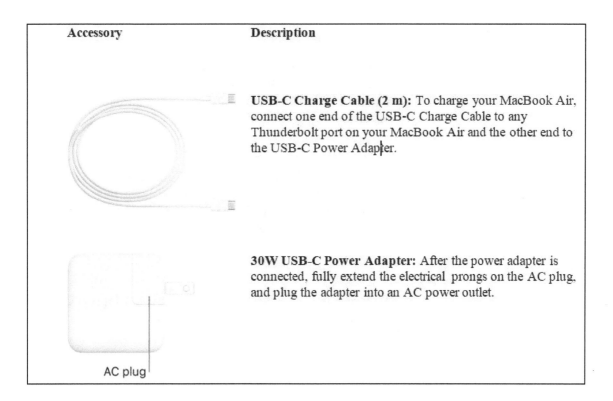

Accessory	Description
	USB-C Charge Cable (2 m): To charge your MacBook Air, connect one end of the USB-C Charge Cable to any Thunderbolt port on your MacBook Air and the other end to the USB-C Power Adapter.
AC plug	**30W USB-C Power Adapter:** After the power adapter is connected, fully extend the electrical prongs on the AC plug, and plug the adapter into an AC power outlet.

To use your MacBook Pro, you require these two included accessories: Other accessories and adapters are sold separately. Review the documentation or contact the manufacturer to ensure that you select the appropriate product.

Apple gives the following accessories for connecting your MacBook Pro to power, external devices, and displays:

Cable or Adapter	Description
	USB-C to USB Adapter: Connect your MacBook Air to standard USB accessories.
	USB-C to Lightning Cable: Connect your iPhone or other iOS or iPadOS device to your MacBook Air for syncing and charging.
	USB-C Digital AV Multiport Adapter: Connect your MacBook Air to an HDMI display, while also connecting a standard USB device and a USB-C charge cable to charge your MacBook Air.
	USB-C VGA Multiport Adapter: Connect your MacBook Air to a VGA projector or display, while also connecting a standard USB device and a USB-C charge cable to charge your MacBook Air.
	Thunderbolt 3 (USB-C) to Thunderbolt 2 Adapter: Connect your MacBook Air to Thunderbolt 2 devices.

CHAPTER 11

HOW TO GET THE BEST FROM YOUR MACBOOK

Apple prides itself on the brilliance and elegance of its software and, on the surface, macOS proves to be an intuitive and easy-to-navigate operating system. However, if you dig deeper, you will find a ton of useful settings and options that you can use to personalize your computing experience. Here are some of our favorites.

1. Turn off Siri

Siri does not have to say your answers aloud; you can display them silently on the screen. If you prefer this option, go to the Apple menu, then System Preferences, and finally Siri. Finally, check the Disable option next to the Voice Annotations heading. You can change other aspects of Siri in the same dialog, such as the voice. Hide the icon in the menu bar or dock if you prefer a less cluttered interface.

2. Simplify Your Internet Vision

The Safari web browser can block ads and other distractions, allowing you to concentrate on the text on a specific page. To begin, launch your browser in order to permanently activate this minimal view reading mode. Next, select Preferences from the Safari menu (located at the top of the screen). Unlock the Reader tab in this system, then find and select the When visiting other websites drop-down list.

3. Distribute Files

If you have an iCloud account, macOS allows you to easily share files with your contacts. Unlock Finder and navigate to the desired file. Click the Share button (it looks like an arrow pointing out of a box) at the top of this Finder window and select Add People. Then, in the following dialog box, you can select your sharing method, the recipients of the file, and whether or not they can make changes to it.

4. Perform a System Configuration Cleanup

The System Preferences application serves as the control panel for all of your Mac's settings and contains dozens of subsections. You can, however, conceal some of these items if you rarely use them. Unlock System preference by launching the application or selecting System preference from the Apple menu at the top of the screen. To see a list of shortcuts, select View from the top bar and then click Personalize. You can now disable menus you don't need to access or restore the items you want to see in the application's main view.

5. Change the travel direction

When you move two fingers across an Apple laptop's track pad, your view scrolls over the open document or website. You can, however, reverse these directions so that moving your fingers down moves the view up. Navigate to the touch panel menu in System Preferences. Select the Pan Direction: Natural checkbox under the Pan and Zoom heading.

6. Verify settings more quickly

Because many of these options were previously accessible via System Preferences, simply launching the application will expedite the customization process. Keep it in the Dock by opening System Preferences, clicking and holding the Dock icon, selecting Options, and then selecting Keep in Dock. You can now quickly launch the application by clicking on the icon, or you can bring up a list of the various setup screens by pressing and holding the icon before opening the application.

CHAPTER 12

BEST TIPS AND TRICKS

At this point, you might have gained a lot of knowledge about navigating through your Mac, as well as taking care of it. In this chapter, you will learn more tips and tricks that will lay a great foundation for you to become an expert in dealing with your Mac. Here are some of the interesting tricks that you will be glad to have come across:

Switch between desktops: If you have multiple desktops, switching between them is simple. Simply hold down the Control button and press the left or right arrow.

Copy links faster in Safari: Press Command and L at the same time to highlight the URL bar. To copy, hold down Command and C.

Quick reference to the dictionary: If you come across a word that you don't understand, highlight it and then press on it with the Force Touch Trackpad. On your screen, a dictionary definition of the highlighted word will appear.

Sign PDF documents: Drag the document to an email message if you want to sign some documents that have been sent to you. A button with a down arrow can be found in the upper right corner. Select Markup. Select the box that looks like a signature. Sign on to the trackpad by clicking Trackpad and then using the mouse. Alternatively, you can write your signature on a white sheet of paper and then capture it with a Webcam. To do so, click Camera to indicate that this is the option you want. Keep the signature for future use.

Make your own keyboard shortcut: You may be accustomed to certain keyboard shortcuts. You can make your own keyboard box with the option to select your preferred application. You will also be asked to select your preferred menu command and keyboard shortcut. Finish by clicking Add, and you're done!

Get access to hidden files in the Finder: There will be no more difficulties in locating the hidden files in Finder. Simply press Cmd, Shift, and the period keys (.).

Resizing a window: There are many other options for resizing a window, but most of them change the proportions of the window. To avoid this issue, hold Shift while resizing the window from the corner or edge. This method resizes the window from the center—interesting, isn't it?

Extending battery life: There are several options available to help you extend the battery life of your Mac. Turning off WiFi and Bluetooth, removing runaway applications, ensuring Spotlight indexing is turned off, lowering screen brightness, and turning off Time Machine are all examples. You can even choose to enable Energy Saver Preferences.

Making an auto-duplicating file: If you want to open a file in duplicate, click it, right-click, and then select Get Info. Check it out at the Stationary Pad Box. When you do this, the file will open a duplicate every time you click it. When working with templates, this comes in handy.

Hiding a window: Hiding a window from your desktop is easier than you think. Simply press Command and H to close the window. Return the hidden window by pressing Command and Tab.

CHAPTER 13
MAINTENANCE AND TROUBLESHOOTING

Troubleshooting Problems Of MacBook

You may encounter issues while working on your MacBook. Continue reading to find solutions to your problems. Additional troubleshooting information can be found in Mac Help.

If your MacBook has a problem, there is usually a simple and quick solution. Consider the circumstances that led to the problem. You can narrow down possible causes and find the answers you need by writing down what you were doing before the problem occurred. Keep in mind:

• The applications you were using when the problem occurred. Problems that are specific to a particular application may indicate that the application is incompatible with the version of Mac OS that is installed on your computer.

• Any newly installed software, particularly software that has added items to the system folder.

Storing your MacBook

If you intend to keep your MacBook for an extended period of time, keep it in a cool place (ideally 22 ° C) and charge the battery to 50 percent. If you are storing your computer for more than five months, you should discharge the battery to around 50%. To maintain battery capacity, charge the battery to 50% capacity every six months.

Keeping Your MacBook Clean

When cleaning the outside of your computer and its components, unplug your MacBook first and then turn it off. After that, clean the outside of the computer with a damp, soft, lint-free cloth. Prevent moisture from entering through cracks. Try not to directly spray fluid on the PC. Aerosol sprays, solvents, and abrasives can all damage the finish.

Cleaning Your MacBook's Screen

To clean the screen of your MacBook, turn it off and unplug it first. Then, using the cleaning cloth that came with your MacBook, wipe the screen. Soak the material in water if necessary. Try not to splash fluid directly on the screen.

CHAPTER 14

FAQS

How To Download Apps On Your Device

Open the App Store.

Browse or search for the application you want to download.

Select the Buy or Price option. You have already purchased or downloaded the app if the Open button appears instead of the price or Get button.

How to Get Apple Books on Your Phone

Choose Apple System Preferences.

Apple ID iCloud can be found in the Apple menu.

Make sure iCloud Drive is selected, then click Options, then Books.

How to Control How Often the Calendar Refreshes

If you want your calendars to sync automatically across all of your devices, or if you prefer to push them manually, you can change the interval between refreshes in your preferences.

Start the Mac Calendar program. It is in your Launchpad if it is not on your dock.

From the main menu, select Calendar.

Choose Settings from the drop-down menu.

Select the Accounts tab.

Select something from the pull-down menu.

Select the desired time frame by clicking on it.

How Do You Block Unwanted FaceTime Calls?

FaceTime allows you to instantly block any caller at any time.

Open FaceTime and sign in with your Apple ID.

Locate the number you want to block, then right-click on it and select Block This Caller.

Right-click on their phone number and select Block This Caller.

How to Take Screenshots on Your Smartphone

You can capture the entire screen or a portion of the screen on your MacBook Pro for sharing or archiving. This can be done with the mouse, trackpad, or shortcut keys. As a result, you can select the method that is most convenient for you when taking screenshots on your Mac.

How to Convert a PDF to a Word Document

During the conversion of a page layout document to a word processing document, any existing objects, including text boxes, are preserved. Text boxes that are layered with objects must have their layering and text wrapping adjusted in the converted document.

Perform one of the following:

Choose File > Convert to Word Processor Format from the menu (from the File menu at the top of your screen).

Select the Document Body checkbox in the Document sidebar after clicking the Document tab.

CONCLUSION

Thank you for reading! If you use your Mac for entertainment, you are more likely to browse through various media such as music, videos, and photos. Not to worry, this book explains how to use these features. You can also share media with others in the manner described.

Please keep in mind that the MacBook Pro is available with or without a touch bar. If you have vision problems, a MacBook with a larger screen is a great option.

If you are staying with children who will access your Mac, you can set up separate accounts for them. This allows you to plan and monitor the types of activities to which the children may be exposed. This safeguards minors against potentially harmful information. On your Mac, you can access a variety of other security features. You can access these through the System Preferences, which is the pane where you can customize your computer's settings to meet your needs and requirements.

In the event that you have problems with your Mac, this book will help you troubleshoot them. For example, if your Wi-Fi appears to be operational, restarting your Mac may resolve the problem. If your device is becoming slower when completing tasks, it may be running out of storage space. Ideas and tips for reclaiming your space were also highlighted, including deleting some files and apps, creating ZIP files, and removing temporary files.

If you are unable to resolve the issues that are interfering with the proper operation of your computer, you may schedule an appointment with the Genius Bar nearest to you. Your device will be checked at the Genius Bar by experts who have been properly trained to do so. Please keep in mind that when you take your Mac to the Genius Bar, you must backup your data. You have several options for backup strategies. Backup tools such as Time Machine, iCloud, and Dropbox are available. Serious problems with your Mac may necessitate a reinstall of macOS. Again, you must backup your data for this measure.

Good luck!

Made in United States
Troutdale, OR
08/05/2024